COPING

with

CHANGE

THE ASSOCIATION OF CHRISTIAN TEACHERS OF WALES,
30, Pontarddulais Road, Penllergaer, Swansea,SA4 1AY

ISBN 0 907517 08 0
First published 1991

This booklet is the substance of the 1989 Annual Lecture of the Association of Christian Teachers of Wales.

Dr. Brian Harris, B.Sc., MBBS, MRC Psych.,DPM is Senior Lecturer and Consultant in Psychological Medicine, Department of Psychological Medicine, University of Wales College of Medicine,Cardiff

Typeset and Printed at
The Doron Press,
14 Greenhalgh Moss Lane,
Bury,
Lancashire

COPING WITH CHANGE

Firstly I would like to take this opportunity of thanking you for inviting me to give this annual lecture to the Association of Christian Teachers. Inevitably I ask myself the question "why me?". Presumably the answer is something like this; firstly I am an Evangelical Christian and material is required which takes such a theological stand, secondly I am a Psychiatrist, and therefore should know something about the theory of coping! but thirdly the changes which are going on within the Health Service surely equal those which are going on in Education! We also are trying to cope at a national level with the implementation of two Government White Papers. At a local level each health authority has recently drawn up its ten year plans (in our particular area resulting in the planned winding down of the Mental Hospital and development of District General Hospital Units). Again, in Psychiatry itself we have the development of Community Services with the major moves away from Hospital type services.

The title of the talk implies the need for something intensely practical arising from sound Theology and distinctive (if needs be) from the Secular approach. I suspect that we will have heard the kind of advice outlined many times, but it is rather like the apostle Paul in Romans Ch7 v18 "To will is present with me but how to perform that which is good I know not"!

Changes

To those of us looking on it is obvious that something must be happening in schools. A quick glance at any daily newspaper brings to one's attention the kind of changes with which teachers are having to cope. Some of the changes of course are encountered in Society in general, others are specific to education. Firstly there is the change in moral values in Society, and in our generation we have seen the discarding of traditional Christian values; 'theft' for example, is a major problem in schools, with the need for pupils always to carry their bags with them from class to class. Again within a couple of decades we have witnessed the rise of phenomena such as "group shoplifting" in the lunch-hour or "pack rapes" in the school yard. Secondly there is the problem of discipline or rather of its disappearance and for better or worse the disappearance in school of corporal punishment. Thirdly there is the disintegration of family life and the slow erosion of the concept of the family (at least in a traditional sense) as the unit of society. Then within education itself there is the change in the education process as formalised in development of the National Curriculum and change to G.C.S.E. courses.

There are changes in the School Governing Systems with an insistence on more parental input; as with Hospitals there is the possibility for schools to "opt out". Attitudes of teachers themselves have changed in terms of ambition and scepticism. We have witnessed within the past generation industrial action which in my experience has been very stressful particularly for a number of Christian school teacher patients. Many of these changes have resulted in a tremendously increased workload with the necessity for excessive homework on the part of the teacher. At the same time there has been a devaluing of the profession in terms of pay. All of these changes are stressful and I observe with interest that in the past six months I have seen three teachers (two Christians) all trying to cope with the stress of change, seeking early retirement on health grounds. I do not believe I had seen one prior to this. Obviously the coping mechanisms of these teachers were not adequate and they were becoming incapacitated by symptoms.

Coping

What do we mean by coping? Dr Gaius Davies in his book "Stress:, the, Challenge to Christian Caring" makes the following observations: ""to cope" is not a biblical word and our English word is probably derived from the French word "coup" indicating a blow!'(1) The new Oxford dictionary definition is, "To be or prove oneself a match for, contend successfully with". He concludes that coping is summarised by the exhortation of the Apostle Paul in 1 Corinthians Ch16 v13 "Watch ye, stand fast in the faith, quit you like men, be strong." All of that is coping in a specifically Christian sense!

Factors affecting coping

Firstly **Age.** There is a balance between inexperience and immaturity on the one hand and the inability to accept change on the other. This can be illustrated from the area of research associated with post-natal depression in that there is a strong association of depressed mood following childbirth with younger mothers and older mothers. In the former case the change in lifestyle associated with the first baby in a young mother, perhaps in her late teens, is obvious, and similarly a mother in her mid to late thirties, particularly if the childbirth interrupts a career, may find difficulties in adjusting.(2) Similarly in the teaching world a young teacher may have the capacity to change but inexperience to deal with it; on the other hand an older teacher may be more mature but also more 'rigid', losing the capacity to accept change and take it.

Secondly, **personality** is of importance particularly in terms of the type of reaction which we give to stress. The introduction of the word "stress" to the whole area of mental health occurred in the 'thirties' and was a term borrowed from Physics.(3) It was used to denote both the stressors and the reaction within an individual. Different personalities react in different ways to stress. The most well known personality typing is probably that of Eysenck who developed the concepts of introversion and extroversion.(4)

The introvert tends to brood and worry in reaction to stress, where as the extrovert would be much more likely to lose his temper and become overtly angry. Both of these normal reactions can become pathological and even totally incapacitating, interfering with lifestyle. Physical symptoms and signs may also develop, e.g. there is a strong association between peptic ulceration and worry.

Personality has also been studied in connection with ischaemic heart disease. Research has shown that so called coronary type A personality is associated with coronary artery disease and Myocardial Infarction. This kind of personality has too many goals and objectives, with excessive 'drive'!(5)

Thirdly, **the amount of change** is important. A certain degree of stress is challenging and is part and parcel of everyday life. This can be pictured in the skier or climber who actually enjoys 'stress', the latter contributing to the 'thrill' of the activity. So it is with life in general; but obviously, situations may arise where the degree of change is so great that even the best adjusted person will crack up.

Then fourthly, there are **constitutional factors** which we all share, regardless of age, and personality. Some classical reactions are well described in the Psalms. Even a cursory examination of certain Psalms indicates that the Psalmist was in a state of depression as he wrote, as evidenced by low mood, pessimism, disturbed appetite, sleep and powers of concentration. In the

Psalmist's case of course the condition was a result of sin but even so the interesting question arises as to how much and to what extent it is healthy (i.e. spiritually) for an individual to find himself in the Psalmist's state and condition. Certainly there should be an element of this experience for all of us, but at what stage have we left the realm of healthy normal Christian experience and entered the realm of morbid introspection and rumination? It is amazing to see the great variety of "symptoms" described in the Bible particularly in Psalms. Psalms 38, 77 and 102 show the Psalmist in a depressed state of mind. The basic reaction of his system to his perception is that which any person might show to a different but depressing perception (loss of a loved one). It is interesting to pick out some of these symptoms and link them to questions on modern psychiatric questionnaires: e.g. Psalm 102 v4 "I forget to eat my food" - "has your appetite got less recently?" - Middlesex Hospital Questionnaire.(6) Psalm 77 v4 "You keep my eyes from closing" - "Can you get off to sleep at the moment?" - Middlesex Hospital Questionnaire Psalm 38 v7 "My back is filled with searing pain" - Hamilton depression questionnaire - question 15, "is the patient complaining of muscle aches and pains and backache?" Psalm 38 v10 "My heart pounds, my strength fails" - "do you often suffer from excessive sweating or fluttering of the heart?" (Middlesex Hospital Questionnaire). There are many other examples such as the Psalmist being too troubled almost to speak (Psalm 77 v 4), possibly even mute - a condition occurring in profound depression.

Simple Practical Advice: Tactics

a) The importance of Sunday as a day of rest cannot be overemphasised and sadly even in evangelical circles the tradition of leaving Sunday free is being eroded. Equally, Sunday should not be totally taken up with "Spiritual Activities". Surely it is right and good and proper that an element of physical rest and relaxation should also be present and the day should not be one round of meetings from dawn to dusk.

b) Continued full involvement with the local church is essential, since for all Christians the church is the God given fellowship for worship, fellowship, prayer and sharing. How often do church activities lose out because school activities take over.

An activity which is totally different from my normal everyday employment can be extremely helpful as a form of relaxation. For myself (a general Psychiatrist seeing adults)it is the children's work! There can be such an appropriate outlet for the stressed teacher!

(c) Planned respite. It is of great importance for an individual coping with the kind of changes which havebeen outlined, to plan well ahead so that holidays really are holidays. The only way in which this can be assured is to plan well ahead into one's diary so that blocks of time are clearly outlined.

(d) Cutting back and learning to say "no" is a lesson which Christians find difficult and has to be balanced against"going the second mile". In this respect, to be assertive is important, since much stress can result from the Christian remaining passive and silent,when he should speak up in a bold but caring way.

(e) Daily relaxation is also of importance and the Christian's devotional times obviously are essential; but in addition exercise and hobbies/reading are the rule. Simple daily re laxation exercises may also be useful to tone down the level of anxiety which wecarry in our personalities and mediated by the sympathetic nervous system..(Fight or flight response!).

Strategy

The question now arises as to how the Christian should attempt to cope amidst all the stresses and strains of life. The answer must be with the "whole man". Paul tells us in Romans 6 v17 that " —— Ye have obeyed from the heart that form of sound doctrine which was delivered you", indicating that when the Romans became Christians the whole of their beings were involved. Dr. Lloyd-Jones points out that the apostle is describing three "parts" to the being of man: "mind", "heart" and "will". The Christian life is one "..... in which one has 'obeyed' - there is the will - 'From the heart' - there is the emotion, the sensibility - 'the form of doctrine' which came to the mind and to the understanding. We see then 'the mind' as the seat of understanding and logic, 'the heart' as the seat of the emotions, and 'the will' as the seat of volition.(7)

Any attempt to cope must therefore involve the whole being of the Christian. This is perhaps most easily seen in terms of his perception ('mind' - in this limited sense). How important it is for us to get our perceptions and cognitions right. To return to the state of the Psalmist, all Christians from time to time experience the kind of "feeling states" which the Psalmist went through. Seeking to help someone or ourselves it should be our aim to get the perceptions right. In fact in Psalm 77 the Psalmist, amazingly, halfway through the Psalm, after bemoaning his state and describing his condition, suddenly changes and exclaims (verse 10) "This is my infirmity; but I will remember the years of the right hand of the most High. I will remember the works of the Lord" - and in quite an amazing way he attempts to change his thinking from that which is negative to that which is positive. I believe that this is the key to the Christian's dilemma. In other words the main remedy to prevent despair, to prevent anxiety, to prevent ambition, to prevent scepticism and to cope with stress is to get things clearly in perspective.

Again in Psalm 11 v3 the Psalmist exclaims: "If the foundations be destroyed, what can the righteous do?" It has been suggested that at this point in time, David may well have been at the court of Saul. Although he had been rightly anointed as the future king of Israel, a tremendous jealousy arose in Saul and he was aiming to kill David. David therefore finds himself in a situation as a young man where the very foundations of life itself were being threatened. Apparently the same root word for foundations is also used in Isaiah 19 verse 10, "And they shall be broken in the purposes thereof". The commentator E.J. Young says concerning this word "—— it is likely that Isaiah uses the word in a general sense to denote all upon which the life of Egypt rests - the foundations. When these are crushed, then life itself which is supported by these pillars must also fail".(8) Seemingly, at the present time, the Word of God, the foundations of society, the values of yesterday etc. are all being threatened and the Christian has to cope. As David, the Christian appeals to the sovereignty of God, "when the foundations be destroyed what can the righteous do?"

The answer is that he gets his perspectives right, he reminds himself of the sovereignty of God. "The Lord is in his holy temple, the Lord's throne is in heaven: his eyes behold, his eyelids try, the children of men".(Psalm 11 v4)

The hymnist Cowper does the same thing. Amidst all his troubles, trials, and tribulations, he is able to write

E'en let the unknown morrow
Bring with it what it may.
It can bring with it nothing
But he will see us through.
Who gives the lilies clothing
Will clothe his people too.

I suppose at the end of the day, the real answer to the Christian teacher trying to cope with stress is that "mind", "heart" and "will" must be involved in his Christian life. He must perceive that whatever happens to him is a part of the plan and purpose of God for his sanctification. Even the current changes are not accidental "..... all things work together for good to them that love God, who are the called according to his purpose" (Romans 8 v28).

But as well as our minds (and that is where we begin), our hearts (the seat of our emotions must be moved), and finally our wills the seat of volition, must be stirred into action.

The New Testament sees "the heart" as the seat of the emotions and in coping with stress, keeping a warm heart is a major problem. After all, the Christian life is much more than simply perception and understanding doctrines. There should be appropriate emotional responses to such truth within us. To return to the hymn of Cowper:-

Sometimes a light surprises
The Christian while he sings,
It is the Lord who rises
With healing in his wings,
When comforts are declining
He grants the soul again,
A season of clear shining
To cheer it after rain.

As Jude says (verse 21) "keep yourselves in the love of God". Under conditions of stress it is the easiest thing in the world to become tired and to allow Christian truth to remain at the level of the intellect and have no effect upon our hearts. It is one thing to believe that all things work together for good to them that love

God, it is another to believe that truth and feel it. Sadly, it is possible for the pressures of the day to erode our prayer times and our Bible study in such a way that they become cold and formal rather than times of communion with God.

Finally "the will" must also be involved. In my personal experience it is the easiest thing in the world to succumb to the temptation of simply being resigned to all the proposed changes in the health service. I should imagine that such a temptation comes the way of teachers. However if our minds and hearts are correctly affected then our wills will be galvanised into action perceiving everything that happens to us as spiritual, rather than separating the spiritual from the secular.

A Christian response then is what is needed and the only way in which this can be done is to take the New Testament principles as outlined.

Are we not all "weighed in the balances and found wanting"? There can be no better way of closing than reminding ourselves again of that exhortation of the Apostle Paul:

1 Corinthians 16 verse 13: "Watch ye, stand fast in the faith, quit you like men, be strong!".

REFERENCES

1. Davies, G. (1988)
   Stress: The Challenge to Christian Caring
   Kingsway Publications, London.

2. Paykel, E.S., Emms, E.M., Fletcher, J., and Rassaby, E.S., (1980)
   Life Events and Social Support in Puerperal Depression
   British Journal of Psychiatry 136, 339 - 346.

3. Selye, H. (1952)
   The Story of the Adaptation Syndrome
   ACTA. Montreal.

4. Eysenck, H.J. and Eysenck S.B.G. (1969)
   The Structure and Measurement of Personality
   Routledge and Kegan Paul, London.

5. Friedman, M. and Rosenman, R.H. (1959)
Association of Specific Overt Behaviour Pattern with Blood and Cardiovascular Findings.
Journal of the American Medical Association 169: 1286- 1296.

6. Crown, S. and Crisp, A.H. (1966)
A Short Clinical Diagnostic Self-Rating Scale for Psycho-Neurotic Patients: The Middlesex Hospital Questionnaire
British Journal of Psychiatry 112, 917 - 923.

7. Lloyd-Jones, D.M. (1972)
Romans: An Exposition of Chapter 6: The New Man
Banner of Truth Trust, London.

8. Young, E.J. (1969)
The New International Commentary on the Old Testament
The Book of Isaiah Volume 2
William B. Eerdmans Publishing Company, Grand Rapids, Michigan.